Meet
Unikitty!

Shari Last

Written and Edited by Shari Last
Senior Editor Tori Kosara
Editor Anant Sagar
Senior Designer Jo Connor
Art Editor Suzena Sengupta
Managing Editors Elizabeth Dowsett,
Chitra Subramanyam
Managing Art Editors Ron Stobbart, Neha Ahuja
Art Director Lisa Lanzarini
DTP Designer Umesh Singh Rawat, Rajdeep Singh
Senior Pre-Production Producer Jennifer Murray
Pre-Production Manager Sunil Sharma
Producer Louise Minihane
Reading Consultant Maureen Fernandes
Publisher Julie Ferris
Publishing Director Simon Beecroft

First published in Great Britain in 2015 by
Dorling Kindersley Limited
80 Strand, London, WC2R 0RL

Copyright © 2015 Dorling Kindersley Limited
A Penguin Random House Company
10 9 8 7 6 5 4 3 2 1
001–280033–Jan/2015

A CIP catalogue record for this book
is available from the British Library.
ISBN: 978-0-24118-602-2

Colour reproduction by Alta Image Ltd. UK
Printed and bound in China by South China Printing Company Ltd.

www.LEGO.com
www.dk.com

A WORLD OF IDEAS:
SEE ALL THERE IS TO KNOW

Contents

Princess Unikitty

Princess Unikitty is
half unicorn, half kitten.
She loves rainbows, butterflies,
flowers and happiness!
Most of all, she loves ideas.
Unikitty is so creative,
she can build anything.

4

5

The Many Faces of
Unikitty

Unikitty is almost always sweet and happy. She has some surprising sides too.

Unikitty

Unikitty is a fun Master Builder who loves being happy. She likes dancing and building colourful things.

Queasy Kitty

When poor Unikitty gets seasick she turns green and her eyes change to brown. Being sick does not make Unikitty happy.

Astro Kitty

Unikitty has a blue spacesuit. She wears it when she goes for a ride in a spaceship.

Biznis Kitty

When Unikitty needs a disguise she dresses up as Biznis Kitty. Unikitty does not know much about business. She can't even spell it!

Angry Kitty

Sometimes Unikitty has an unhappy thought and she becomes Angry Kitty. Angry Kitty is very strong and loves protecting her friends.

Master Builder

Master Builders are the best
builders in the universe!
Using their imagination,
they can create anything.

Unikitty builds crazy, colourful things, like catapults that fire brightly coloured flower fireworks.

Unikitty's Building Secrets

I like to build using different coloured bricks.

All my creations are happy and fun like me.

I add colourful objects like stars and wheels to the things I build.

I like to decorate everything with flowers and butterflies. They make me smile.

I built some flower fireworks using see-through pieces.

Welcome to Cloud Cuckoo Land

Unikitty lives in Cloud Cuckoo Land, a wonderful world at the top of a rainbow. There are no rules here – no bedtimes, no baby-sitters and no frowns!

Crazy Castle

Unikitty's magical castle is built using all kinds of wonderful and happy things.

The Sun
It keeps the castle bright, warm and happy.

Flower firework
Even if it hits you, you'll smell lovely.

Catapult
Fling the flower fireworks really far. Look out snail!

Striped pillar

Happy snail

Pink dome
A pretty roof to cover my castle.

Blue flower
Everything looks prettier with flowers.

Star

Pinwheel
Twirls around in the wind. Yay!

15

Happy Thoughts

Unikitty likes to be happy,
happy, happy all the time.
She thinks everyone should
be friendly to each other.
Unikitty pushes away unhappy
thoughts by thinking of nice
things, like candy floss. Yum!

What Makes Me Happy

Happy thoughts

Rainbows

Building fun things

Marshmallows

Flowers

Butterflies

Candy floss

Friends

Creativity

Puppies

Dancing

What Makes Me Angry

Rules

Bedtime

Baby-sitters

Bossy people

Lord Business

Frowns

Rainy days

Dark colours

Bullies

Bushy moustaches

Furballs

Unikitty's New Friends

Hooray! Some new friends have arrived in Cloud Cuckoo Land! Unikitty cannot wait to say hello.

Wyldstyle, Batman, Emmet
and Vitruvius are looking
for more Master Builders.
Unikitty is happy to help!

MEET THE MASTER BUILDERS

Wyldstyle
The Rebel

- Streetwise Master Builder
- Loves being creative
- Built a cool black and orange motorcycle

Emmet
The Special

- Construction worker from Bricksburg
- Loves to make his friends happy
- Built a blue double-decker couch

Benny
The Astronaut

- Spaceman from the 1980s
- Loves spaceships
- Built a spaceship to escape from Lord Business

MetalBeard
The Pirate Captain

- Brave Master Builder
- Likes his pirate ship *The Sea Cow*
- Rebuilt his own body

Vitruvius
The Wizard

- Wise old wizard
- Likes playing the piano
- Built a walker to fight evil robots

Batman
The Superhero

- Heroic Master Builder
- Likes to work alone
- Built a Batmobile out of pieces from a Batplane

A New Threat

President Business is
a super cool guy.
Or so everyone thinks…

But secretly he is
Lord Business.
He wants to
stop imagination
and ban ideas!
He plans to glue
everything together
so it can never
be changed again!

25

A Master Plan

Unikitty takes her friends to a meeting with all the Master Builders on Cloud Cuckoo Land. It is time to stop Lord Business! Is Emmet the Special, the one who has the power to save the world?

Poor Queasy Kitty

After escaping Lord Business's attack on Cloud Cuckoo Land, Unikitty and her friends become lost at sea.

Luckily Emmet had built a
double-decker couch to float
on, which saves them all.
But poor Unikitty starts feeling
a bit seasick.

Rescued!

Unikitty does not have
to be queasy any more.
Brave pirate MetalBeard sails
to the rescue on his pirate ship.
Now Unikitty can
be her happy self
once again!

31

Unikitty Means Biznis

To help her friends stop Lord Business, Unikitty is disguised as Biznis Kitty. With drawn-on glasses and a tie, she hopes no one will realise that she knows nothing about business.

"Business, business, business... numbers! YAY!"

Brave Biznis Kitty helped stop Lord Business's evil plans. We caught up with her for an interview.

What was the plan to stop Lord Business?

Emmet's super duper plan was for me to distract Lord Business

Talking
BIZNIS

Saving the world, one meeting at a time

so that the others could stop his plan. I kept him busy by talking about business, but we all got caught. I was very sad!

What did you do then?

We escaped from Lord Business's evil lair in a spaceship.

We zoomed straight to the city to stop Lord Business's evil plan.

Do you really know a lot about business?

I know lots about business. Business, business, business... numbers! YAY! Business is so much fun. I get very distracted and forget about everything else!

5-4-3-2-1...
Astro Kitty

Benny the Spaceman
builds a spaceship
to help in the
battle against Lord Business.

Unikitty puts on her blue
spacesuit and joins him on board.
She is excited to go into space!

Watch Out for Angry Kitty!

Every once in a while, an unhappy idea might still be a good one! When Unikitty's friend Emmet is in trouble, she turns into Angry Kitty, and joins in the fight!

Angry Kitty Saves Bricksburg

By a Bricksburg special reporter

A celebration turned into a dangerous battle yesterday.

Lord Business wanted to freeze everyone in the town of Bricksburg, using his robots, the scary Micro Managers.

They were capturing people and gluing them in place!

Hope seemed lost until Angry Kitty and her friends came to the rescue. *Boom, crash, ka-pow!*

THE BRICKSBURG
TIMES

"Mess with the cat, you get the horns!"

The Micro Managers couldn't escape Angry Kitty as she zoomed around breaking them into little pieces.

The brave Angry Kitty defeated all the Micro Managers and saved the town.
She is a hero.

Happy Unikitty

Unikitty has helped
to save the world.
What a happy thought!

She dances and laughs
with all her friends.
Now she can go
back to being
happy again!

Glossary

Ban
Put a stop to something

Creative
Using your own ideas to
think of new things

Double-decker
Something that has two levels

Imagination
The part of the mind that
thinks up creative ideas

Queasy
Feeling a bit sick

Spacesuit
A special outfit
designed to keep
you safe in space

Index

Guide for Parents

DK Reads is a three-level reading series for children, developing the habit of reading widely for both pleasure and information. These books have exciting running text interspersed with a range of reading genres to suit your child's reading ability, as required by the school curriculum. Each book is designed to develop your child's reading skills, fluency, grammar awareness and comprehension in order to build confidence and engagement when reading.

Ready for a *Beginning to Read* book
YOUR CHILD SHOULD

- be using phonics, including combinations of consonants, such as bl, gl and sm, to read unfamiliar words; and common word endings, such as plurals, ing, ed and ly.

- be using the storyline, illustrations and the grammar of a sentence to check and correct their own reading.

- be pausing briefly at commas, and for longer at full stops; and altering his/her expression to respond to question, exclamation and speech marks.

A Valuable and Shared Reading Experience

For many children, reading requires much effort but adult participation can make this both fun and easier. So here are a few tips on how to use this book with your child.

TIP 1 Check out the contents together before your child begins:

- Read the text about the book on the back cover.
- Read through and discuss the contents page together to heighten your child's interest and expectation.
- Briefly discuss any unfamiliar or difficult words on the contents page.

- Chat about the non-fiction reading features used in the book, such as headings, captions, recipes, lists or charts.

This introduction helps to put your child in control and makes the reading challenge less daunting.

TIP 2 Support your child as he/she reads the story pages:

- Give the book to your child to read and turn the pages.
- Where necessary, encourage your child to break a word into syllables, sound out each one and then flow the syllables together. Ask him/her to reread the sentence to check the meaning.
- When there's a question mark or an exclamation mark, encourage your child to vary his/her voice as he/she reads the sentence. Demonstrate how to do this if it is helpful.

TIP 3 Praise, share and chat:

- The factual pages tend to be more difficult than the story pages, and are designed to be shared with your child.
- Ask questions about the text and the meaning of the words used. Ask your child to suggest his/her own quiz questions. These help to develop comprehension skills and awareness of the language used.

A FEW ADDITIONAL TIPS

- Try and read together every day. Little and often is best. After 10 minutes, only keep going if your child wants to read on.
- Always encourage your child to have a go at reading difficult words by themselves. Praise any self-corrections, for example, "I like the way you sounded out that word and then changed the way you said it, to make sense."
- Read other books of different types to your child just for enjoyment and information.

Have you read these other great books from DK?

BEGINNING TO READ

Holly's dream has come true – she is given her very own puppy!

Meet the animals of Heartlake City and their cheerful, fun-loving owners.

Join the wacky Mixels™ as they have fun, play pranks – and mix!

STARTING TO READ ALONE

School is out and the girls of Heartlake City are off on their latest adventures!

Follow Laval the lion and his friends on their dangerous quests across Chima™.

Zoe shares the thrill of her travels across the Amazon rainforest.